LITERATURE IS A VOYAGE OF DISCOVERY

LITERATURE IS A VOYAGE OF DISCOVERY

TOM BISHOP
IN CONVERSATION WITH
DONATIEN GRAU

DIAPHANES

For more than half a century, Tom Bishop had the reputation of hold-ing sway over the interactions between Paris and New York. This reign extended not only to the domains of literature and philosophy—students gathered at New York University for more than twenty years to hear the words of the invited professor and theoretician of the Nouveau Roman Alain Robbe-Grillet—but also to the humanities as a whole. Tom has a vision of the university within the city, as a microcosm and a high-stakes encounter with all the city contains. His actions at NYU marked a time when Paris counted more than other cities, and New York was becoming the new great global center of culture. Tom belongs to the era of world capitals, the era of the *translatio culturae* that took place between Paris and New York, though Paris was still the principal source of inspiration.

When I met Tom in 2010, I was immediately struck by his force of character, his vital energy. At the time, I was caught up in a few disagree-ments at the École Normale Supérieure where I was teaching. No sooner had I mentioned this in confidence to Tom than he said: "But then come and give a lecture here!" That's how, at the age of twenty-four, I found myself invited to give a Florence Gould Lecture—the lecture series over which Tom had final say. I devoted my talk to some research in progress on Proust and Sainte-Beuve.

And so our friendship began: after that lecture, Tom invited me to organize a discussion on "Art Spaces" with Philippe de Montebello, Joachim Pissarro, and Philippe Vergne, the three great French figures of the New York art world. Then Tom and I co-organized the confer-ence *Re-Thinking Literature*, held at NYU in 2013. When Tom offered that we plan his annual conference at the Center for French Civilization and Culture together, I knew immediately that we had continue to do what he had been doing all along: to confront the big questions, with rigor and audacity, in full knowledge that what has been done so far is only a beginning, a starting point. This conference gave rise to a volume, *Ways of Re-Thinking Literature*, that was conceived between New York and Paris, and that one dreams of seeing prolonged in a multiplicity of other books, from the perspectives of Delhi, Lagos, Shanghai, Kuala Lumpur, Mexico City, or Buenos Aires.

In speaking with Tom, I wanted to let people hear his voice, the voice of a scholar, a figure of our time, so intensely alive. The conversations collected here arose from various situations over the course of the past four years. Tom Bishop speaks of aspects of his research and retraces his own journey, his story: his departure from Vienna as a child—he now calls himself "a non-Viennese, non-Jewish Viennese Jew"—his studies, his encounters, his choices, his roles, his conceptions of literature and of life, his relationships with the worlds of politics and economics. He speaks of how he contributed to defining the profession of *curator* as it is practiced today, all while preferring by far the vocation of professor. We see the scholar, the organizer, the major figure of intellectual life, and also the person, with his affirmations, his rage, his refusals, his loyalty, his insatiable appetite for discovery and for that which is new. And we see his deep attachment to the university, a place of liberty and creation.

Donatien Grau

First takes

DONATIEN GRAU: Tom, you have given your life to literature, to a certain idea of literature. I feel there's a starting point to this journey: when you were nine years old, you left Austria in 1938 and came to Paris without knowing French. You learned French on your own at the Lycée Janson de Sailly, where—though you didn't know it at the time—you were classmates with a boy whose itinerary was the same as yours: George Steiner.

Within a few months you mastered French, only to leave again in June 1940, on the last boat setting out for the United States. Could you tell me about your relationship to literature in these three languages: German, which is the language you were born into, French, and English?

TOM BISHOP: German will go the quickest, because I have a rejection of German. I don't have a habit of speaking German, or at any rate I didn't keep the habit for very long. That has fallen away a bit since I was nine. I made my peace with the German language quite a long time ago. German, for me, was my native language, obviously, so it was the language I spoke at home, with my parents.

But my relationship to it has been conditioned by history.

This was in Austria in 1938—that is, at the moment of the *Anschluss*, the moment when Austria was reclaimed by the Germans. I'm not sure *reclaim* is the right word, but that's how it felt at the time. My family was Viennese. I would write anti-German poems. My family thought I had a very materialistic side, because I used to sell these poems to my family members, taking into account what each of them could afford. It wasn't that I particularly wanted to write in German: it was the only language I had. I didn't know any others.

In late 1938, we left Vienna for Budapest, illegally in fact. German was a kind of imaginary space, like literature, like poetry: it wasn't made for a nine-year-old child, but I was already reading a lot in my parents' library. I took to it, and writing these anti-German poems became an absolute necessity.

DG: Anti-German poems, in German?

TB: Yes, truly in German, with the knowledge I had of the language and its poetry. I have a precise memory of the *Anschluss*. Afterward, we went to Budapest and then on to Paris. We weren't allowed to stay in Budapest. We passed through Austria, through Germany, to Paris. Everything was changing vertiginously fast.

I left Vienna fifteen days after the *Anschluss*… *Anschluss*, that word was anathema to all the… I almost said to all the Austrians, but who were the Austrians? The morning after the *Anschluss*—it happened on a Friday night, the Austrian government conceded, threw in the towel—the morning after, all of Vienna, I saw it, I was nine years old, all of Vienna was covered in swastikas, covered in huge German flags that the Austrians loved. Everything was in place, everything was ready to be hung up on Ringstrasse, on all the streets of Vienna. They didn't lose a minute; it was immediate. To me who loved Austria… Why did I love Austria? I didn't know any better. We saw things happen remarkably swiftly, everything turned upside down in twenty-four hours, the German invasion happened, swift and very violent.

What did I know, personally? I didn't know much. I knew enough to know that the Germans were the ones in charge now: I didn't need much schooling to learn that. It was clear, very clear. Anyone with their eyes open could see what was happening in a country that, ten days earlier, had been more or less a free country. I say "more or less" because freedom in Austria was relative—fairly relative. It was relative just about everywhere.

DG: You came to Paris, and you had to speak French, a language you didn't know.

TB: I didn't know a word of French. I had an aunt who lived in Paris: she was my uncle's wife. My uncle was Hungarian—my entire family on my mother's side was Hungarian. The Austrians, whom you couldn't call Austrians anymore, had been swept aside.

These past few years, I've wondered a lot about what I knew at the time, what I was conscious of at the time. What did I know? Not many things, but enough to make myself understood during the handful of days I spent living in a country that was now occupied, that had been subjected to an occupation that was evil, but that the Austrians didn't view as evil. A majority of them were delighted. I still have those images in my mind's eye, of the German army passing through the wide streets of Vienna to such applause as we could have hardly imagined. For someone like me, who was writing anti-German poems, it was hard to believe, or even impossible to believe: the Austrians had forgotten who they were… It wasn't only the very, very, very strong antisemitism; the whole country had become fascist, Nazi. There was really nothing left of what Vienna had been.

My world became smaller and smaller by the hour, and the Nazi attacks began almost immediately. It was a very, very, difficult period. I didn't know a thing, and it was very painful to be a German-speaking anti-Nazi.

DG: German-speaking and German-hating.

TB: Both. It was very painful.

DG: When you came to Paris, you developed a passion for the French language and for French literature, like a new birth.

TB: Yes, it was very much a new birth: French replaced German for me, but I had to learn it first; I didn't know the least thing about it.

DG: Speaking of which, you had a schoolmate whom you didn't know, but whose life has strange parallels with your own: George Steiner.

TB: Yes, that's true. George Steiner and I crossed the Atlantic at the same time. We came to America at the same moment, on the same ship, the *Champlain*, which was torpedoed on its return voyage. We disembarked in New York, and the ship set out for France again and was torpedoed and sank, of course. George Steiner was at Janson de Sailly at the same time I was, having come from Vienna as I did, and having been raised in approximately the same milieu. And yet we never consciously crossed paths with each other...

DG: You devoted yourself to studying French, the language and the literature...

TB: Literature came a little later: first the language. I was enormously attracted to the language, not only because it is a beautiful language, but also because it wasn't the language of the Germans—that was the most important thing for me.

DG: What spurred you to dedicate your life to French literature and culture?

TB: I remember those days at a French school. I was spurred to use French. They called me a kraut—me, who hated Germany... I had arrived mid-year; I didn't speak French. Within six months, I was on the honor roll; within a year, I was on the high honor roll. That shows you how strong a spur it was: to get people to stop calling me a kraut, and to excel in a language that had become my new home.

The French language was given to me as a gift, in a sense. I couldn't have foreseen I'd use it to turn against the German language.

DG: And English?

TB: It was too soon for English; I didn't know anything yet. It took time. One doesn't learn straight off, but I began studying English at the Petit Lycée, at Janson de Sailly.

DG: And afterward, 1940, New York? The Lycée Français?

TB: I didn't go to the Lycée Français de New York. I went to an American school where I found myself with children from all over Europe, and we learned English together.

But the most important thing for me was my brother, Émile. I had an elder brother, a brother who was four years older than I was, and he looked a lot more than four years older. I was twelve at the time. He was sixteen. He looked eighteen, twenty. I greatly admired him.

When we arrived in France, we decided to speak French with each other, as a defense against German. My brother was absolutely with me, and I was absolutely with him. Both of us were passionately anti-German, anti "German Austria."

When we got to New York, we had to speak English, but between ourselves we spoke exclusively in French. He had served in the Free French Forces… We continued speaking French to each other all our lives. It was essential to have this space where we could exist among ourselves, a language.

French wasn't just a language, it had become our language, a defense against everything that was attacking us. I was able to keep my French thanks to my brother. He spoke it well. He was already sixteen, very talented. He continued on purpose, because he didn't want me to lose the language. And as a result, I still have it today.

All the while that I was becoming American—and fully American too, as I still am today—I kept this space of the French language in which I read continuously. At the age of sixteen, seventeen, I was reading the great French classics, and that's how, in a very natural way, a possible profession opened up for me.

DG: In your work at NYU, you sought to establish a canon, as it were.

TB: I'm not sure I'd say *establish*. To transcribe a canon, yes. You're attributing to me a vocation that I don't necessarily have… To be Franco-American in literature during the 1950s, 1960s, was an interesting position to be in: the French novel was deeply inspired by the American novel, and the French novel was radically new.

DG: And so you chose Robbe-Grillet, inviting him to teach at NYU, every year for thirty years.

TB: I don't think one can say in such clear-cut terms that I "chose Robbe-Grillet." It's more complicated than that: I thought Claude Simon was as great as Robbe-Grillet, if not greater, and I even invited him to NYU, long before he won the Nobel. Unfortunately, he didn't really accept to teach; he was too shy.

But I didn't ask myself who was 'the greatest.' The important thing was to have writers here who had invented a new way of reading, a new way of writing, hitherto unseen. The idea worked; it caught on.

DG: You took an interest in autofiction…

TB: Yes, the authors invented the trends. Camille Laurens, Hélène Cixous, Catherine Millet, of course, wrote these books and invented a new kind of writing, unprecedented. One can find equivalents in the United States, authors who came and spoke at the conference we organized at NYU in fact, like Siri Hustvedt and Daniel Mendelsohn.

The word *autofiction* itself was coined by my colleague Serge Doubrovsky. Doubrovsky was a great figure. He was someone who marked the literature of his time. Not only did he write exemplary works in a practice that was about to become widespread. He also named it. Each time we use the word autofiction we are, so to speak, indebted to Doubrovsky, who is much better known in America for his research on Proust than for his own novels. Autofiction was an important new form that had equivalents in the United States. It made its way and marked French literature over a fairly long period, and in a sense it continues today.

DG: I'd also like to ask you about the relationship between the worlds of Paris and New York. I feel that you belong to an epic era, perhaps now ended, an era when all things were decided at the Café de Flore and the Brasserie Lipp in Paris—where you are still known as the *Loup Blanc*— and at the Café Loup in New York, or even at Knickerbocker's... What's your perspective on the social life of that world. Did these poles of influence exist, or were they already fictions?

TB: No, no, I think you're right these poles existed, and they were strong focal points, intellectually, socially, artistically. We were speaking of Robbe-Grillet. He became, or even partly made himself, the most important figure of all these writers, the one who was most read, best known. But he needed readers to read him. That was the case with Nathalie Sarraute as well, but perhaps not with Robert Pinget in the same way, though he was an important author too. There was a kind of Zeitgeist.

DG: To use a German word…

TB: I knew you'd catch that. But the Zeitgeist counted a lot, and, to come back to your question, this was also a milieu: there were friendships, encounters. People began reading and buying Robbe-Grillet only a short time after he started writing: it worked. He was also a society figure; one can't deny it. He became very famous very quickly. No one had to invent any mechanisms; they took shape automatically. And the world of French letters was immensely impressed. There was an audience that was ready to read in French, after World War II, and that wanted to get its hands on something new.

DG: You were very strongly associated with the Nouveau Roman. Could you tell me what interested you about the movement?

TB: Among writers, a few figures were calling for a "new novel." It caught on, and it began to work. The United States was a natural place for the Nouveau Roman to work—even the name itself was perfect. Publishers like Grove Press printed a lot of them.

DG: What made it so fitting?

TB: Because America wanted to think new, wanted to make it new, and you didn't need to convince the writers of the Nouveau Roman to make it new—that's how they thought, and that's how they worked, whether it was Nathalie Sarraute or Marguerite Duras, or Robbe-Grillet of course.

No one had read anything like Robbe-Grillet before Robbe-Grillet, no one had seen that kind of literature, the techniques he used, and no one had seen anything like the writing of Nathalie Sarraute either. They were new attempts, with ideas that may not have been very conceptualized at first, but they became so, later. They knew where they wanted to go.

DG: You forged connections among various fields and schools of thought: today, there's a tendency to map literature out, to define the schools of thought. A person has to be on one side or the other. People choose their battles and leave the rest aside. It seems to me that your era—and your vision—were much more transversal.

TB: Listen, to be simplistic about it… The fields were there for the taking. When you have a writer who is starting to write a new kind of novel—what would later come to be called the Nouveau Roman—like Robbe-Grillet, for instance, it's relatively easy to say "this interests us," "this matters to us." For Nathalie Sarraute's readers, as for Alain Robbe-Grillet's readers, everything was there for the taking: it was new; it was intelligent; it had a potential readership; and this readership expanded rapidly thanks to the publishing houses, thanks to a lot of things that came together to make it all work.

DG: We haven't spoken of the French trend in the humanities known as *les sciences humaines*, which you took a deep interest in as well.

TB: Yes, it's true that, alongside philosophy—or 'theory,' as we called it—a whole field of absolutely thrilling research was taking place in the humanities. There was the work of my friend Edgar Morin, one of the greats, at once a sociologist and a systematic thinker. A true humanist. But there was also the whole school of history and politics that I closely followed during the 1970s, with François Furet and Emmanuel Le Roy Ladurie. It was all happening at the same time.

DG: There was a time when people said—and some authors still hold this against you, in fact—that all it took for someone to make a name for themselves in the United States was an invitation from Tom Bishop. What do you think of that mythology?

TB: I don't believe a word of it. I think that, to make a name for yourself as a writer, you have to have something to offer your readers. And that was the case. But it wasn't always the case in the same way. Nathalie Sarraute's readers weren't necessarily the same as Robbe-Grillet's—in fact, they usually weren't. But a person like Hélène Cixous is very interesting in this regard. A writer like Nathalie Sarraute was relatively easy to understand, so she didn't need an intermediary for her books to be read, accepted, bought. It worked.

DG: And Hélène Cixous?

TB: Hélène Cixous was much more difficult, from a commercial standpoint. But from a human or literary standpoint, she was just as important, and she had just as significant an impact. One can truly say that she changed the American literary and philosophical landscape. Hélène Cixous never worked *as* Robbe-Grillet worked. She worked just fine *as* Hélène Cixous, an immense writer who reached an audience in the United States that was different from her audience in France. And this continued, in fact. With Hélène, and also with Susan Sontag, we were among the first to organize a conference on feminism, in the 1970s. We also celebrated a new generation of women writers in the 1990s, including Marie NDiaye, Linda Lê.

DG: How would you describe the process of these invitations?

TB: They weren't separate moments, they were a whole set of things that worked, and I think this whole set is what succeeded in finding readers, in being seen.

DG: Tom, it's clear that you are a professor who has conducted research, worked, and written, and at same time you are a person who knows many people and has the knack of bringing all these things together: the people you know, your writing and the university, and the literary and artistic life.

TB: Do I really have the knack of it? I don't know. But that's how it all happened, that's how it all came about, without my really wanting it, without my knowing it.

What happened
to the avant-garde?

DG: One topic I wanted to discuss with you is the avant-garde, which, I know, has been a central focus of your work. I feel you would have some compelling statements to make for today...

TB: The avant-garde was omnipresent not long ago. It's hard to find today. Maybe the avant-garde has disappeared, or maybe it's just hibernating. For a large part of the 20th century, literature was profoundly influenced by the inventions, innovations, and discoveries of avant-garde movements, more at some times than others, more in some countries than others, but it was always present. Many of the most interesting, and certainly the most exciting, artistic creations during a significant part of the 20th century were either part of the avant-garde movements of the time or were directly influenced by them.

Avant-garde movements tend to appear and remain for a period of time and then be followed either by a period of absorption into the mainstream or by a period of reaction against. Both phenomena are cyclic, but the strength and duration of the cycles varies greatly; in the 20th century, avant-garde movements tended to be strong and to remain active for a relatively long time, so that one can reasonable think of it as a century of the avant-garde. Or perhaps, to be more precise, that was true for about three-fourths or perhaps even four-fifths of the century, but in the final years of the 20th and these early years of the 21st century the avant-garde seems, on the whole, remarkably silent.

DG: What do you make of the term *avant-garde*?

TB: So much has been written about the avant-garde that the very expression has become suspect. It's difficult to pin it down because you can't have a universal definition applicable to all forms of art and to all eras. For some, the idea of the avant-garde is limited to what is daring—even though today "daring" applies only to the work whereas, during the Belle Époque and even afterwards, it also applied to the personal behavior of the artist who tried to shock the middle class: "épater les bourgeois." Ubu's "Merdre!" defied acceptable stage discourse, but deliberately outrageous public behavior could be equally shocking and provocative. Perhaps the most celebrated incitement to an entire generation's avant-garde aesthetic was Diaghilev's quasi-order to Jean Cocteau, "Étonne-moi"—"Astonish me." Never mind that Diaghilev was busy talking to Nijinsky and threw out this challenge to shut the very young Cocteau up—at least temporarily. But Cocteau did in fact turn the injunction to astonish into the cornerstone of his life-long ambition to be an avant-garde artist; he in fact succeeded in becoming one for more than a decade, though not beyond that.

The call to astonish, which also inspired many other writers and plastic artists of the 20s, could, of course, lead to trendiness, and some people have compared the avant-garde to fashion—as if the spirit of the avant-garde were somehow linked to the psychology of the high-fashion industry. In 1923, the great director Charles Dullin touched on the willingness, or unwillingness, of audiences to accept new modes: "In the theater, as in all the arts, there are those who can see and those who are born blind. The latter require an entire lifetime to get used to great things and it is only after having heard it said over and over for fifty years that something is beautiful that they yield to the judgment of others."

DG: How can one hope to find a global definition of the avant-garde when it isn't even easy to say what it is at any one time in any one field?

TB: It might be easier to approach the problem negatively, by considering that the essence of the avant-garde is opposed to the essence of what is currently acceptable to the establishment, even to the best of the establishment, *especially* to the best. Both in the past and in the present, the avant-garde—whether in theater, the novel, poetry, ballet, music or painting—represents above all a reaction against the established forms in each of these fields. These reactions take on different shapes in different eras and might have nothing more in common than their opposition to the established order. If, for instance, the current mode of literary expression is Realism, then the avant-garde will tend to be anti-Realist. If, on the other hand, it is Symbolism, then the avant-garde will be anti-Symbolist. As a mode approaches its zenith, it becomes formulaic and arbitrary and begins to lose contact with the artistic aspirations of a younger generation. For the experimentalist, any current mode is already degenerating.

The avant-garde artist is a revolutionary who wages a continuous minority struggle against the artistic forms generally appreciated by others. But these 'others' are not the easily satisfied public of boulevard theater or pulp fiction; rather, the avant-garde writer takes issue with literate writers who attract a large, literate public. For example, the theater of a Beckett or a Genet does not stand in opposition to the light entertainments of a Marcel Achard. It stands in opposition to the intellectual plays of Anouilh or Giraudoux. That's the only way that the military metaphor inherent in the expression "avant-garde" makes sense. The small advance guard of an army prepares the terrain for the main body of troops; similarly, avant-garde writers, when they are successful, show the way not for mere commercialism but for those serious writers to come who will later command a large public.

DG: Does that mean that the avant-garde, when it exists, necessarily embodies what is most substantive in an art form?

TB: By its very nature, it is an aesthetic-in-the-making rather than one already constituted. It's a 'becoming' which not everyone feels comfortable with, even among the most refined critics. For example, in 1971, at the height of Tel Quel and Deconstruction, Roland Barthes was reticent, even pessimistic vis-à-vis the avant-garde of the absurd; only Brecht's political theater could find favor in his eyes. Barthes himself described his theoretical position candidly, perhaps not realizing its surprising weakness: "My own theoretical position is to be in the rear-guard of the avant-garde," he wrote. Antoine Compagnon was quite right to include Barthes among his "anti-moderns."

DG: What happens to the avant-garde once it exists then?

TB: It becomes necessarily subject to the laws of artistic evolution. An avant-garde can never remain an avant-garde for long, since it defines itself in relationship to the current establishment which itself changes constantly. And so it is either rejected or absorbed. If an avant-garde fails (and that is the fate of most), it generally disappears without leaving any trace. But if it manages to impose itself, it eventually changes the current "establishment" or accepted forms. Its influence varies depending on the circumstances: it might be limited to some new techniques, or it might be much more extensive, as was the case with Surrealism, for instance, which imposed a new aesthetic with far-reaching implications, all the way down to advertising.

The very expression *avant-garde* is necessarily restricted to relatively few writers or artists who, at least at first, have only a limited influence. It's a minority thrust that cannot enter the mainstream without ceasing to be experimental. When an avant-garde movement becomes fashionable, its revolutionary value is already spent. At that point, having attained its goal of reform, the avant-garde becomes part of the establishment; it will ultimately inspire new avant-gardes which will rise to oppose the 'tyranny' that it has itself become, in a perpetual cyclical movement.

DG: You are a specialist of the Theater of the Absurd. What do you make of it in the avant-garde context?

TB: No so very long ago, during that extraordinary explosion of creative theatrical innovation in the 1950s, the very notion of the avant-garde, which had played such a large part in the aesthetics of French art in all its varied forms since the middle of the nineteenth century, finally triumphed in the theater with Ionesco, Beckett, Genet, and Adamov. They radically changed theater, first in France and soon throughout the Western world. This was an iconoclastic avant-garde, that sought to change the rules of the game, to radicalize theatricality, to do away with what was left of realistic techniques after half a century of brilliant anti-realist reactions against the successful fourth-wall Realist brainwashing initiated by André Antoine and his Théâtre Libre in the 1890s—itself an avant-garde in its time, and a wildly successful one.

And this Nouveau Théâtre was an immensely successful avant-garde. Word went out from the little Left Bank play-houses that new concepts of theatricality were downgrading the mainstays of even the best playwrights of the time (Sartre, Camus, Montherlant, Anouilh)—namely, plot, character, psychology, coherent stories. The new playwrights didn't offer a common vision; what united them to some extent though was their opposition to the status quo. Soon they were being performed in larger, more important theaters, like the Odéon and eventually the Comédie Française, and they became *the* playwrights of the 50s and 60s. It's rare for an avant-garde to impose itself so thoroughly, and for the experimentalists in revolt to become so quickly the established figures of an art form. But that is, astonishingly, what happened with what came to be known, for better or worse, as the Theater of the Absurd.

Serious playwrights could legitimately claim that one could no longer write theater as before. Obviously, some dramatists *did* continue to write theater as before, just as many twentieth-century novelists continued to produce good or bad nineteenth-century novels, as if Joyce, Kafka, Virginia Woolf, Beckett, Borges, and the Nouveau Roman had never existed. But for those who thought seriously about the stage, the Parisian avant-garde of the 1950s had shattered the mold and made it impossible to go back to even the best of former models. It also revealed a new, serious problem.

Ionesco, in his brilliant definition of the avant-garde, had warned that as soon as an avant-garde is successful enough to become the new establishment, it necessarily engenders its own reaction, another avant-garde which, in turn, seeks to destroy and replace it. However, following its fifteen or twenty years of undisputed triumph, the avant-garde of the absurd yielded not to new writing but, in France at least, to the reign of the director.

DG: You once said: "To write as before after Ioneso was difficult, after Beckett, impossible." What does that mean?

TB: The towering figures, Beckett, Ionesco, Genet, remained; others faded or disappeared. A few important playwrights, like Fernando Arrabal and Michel Vinaver, have continued right up to the present time creating absurdist-related yet highly idiosyncratic works. No powerful group emerged to take the lead; some splendid writers did turn to the stage but at no point did they form anything resembling an avant-garde movement. Among the best of these, in France, were Nathalie Sarraute, Marguerite Duras, Copi, Hélène Cixous, Valère Novarina, followed by Xavier Durringer, Bernard-Marie Koltès, Philippe Minyana, Yasmina Reza.

The only 'movement' to speak of was the brief period of success in the 70s and 80s of the "Théâtre du Quotidien." This was led by several French authors who refocused attention, however briefly, on the text and with it, on the preeminence of the dramatist. They dealt with the things of everyday life, especially in the lives of simple, inarticulate people, thus implying a social critique while eschewing Brechtian didacticism. Most notably, the Théâtre du Quotidien was the first important movement on the French stage since 1900 to go against the almost continuous, century-long reaction against theatrical realism, or against what one critic called "the flight from naturalism." If this new movement, late in the century, didn't revert to truly outmoded nineteenth-century forms of theatricality, it certainly didn't point to a new, experimental direction either, and it didn't herald some new avant-garde.

DG: Is there a specificity of French theater for each period?

TB: Not all directors possess as great a power of imagination, nor the same means to express it. The French directors of the 80s, on the whole, followed analogous paths, preferring the classics to contemporary authors, famous authors' lesser-known works to their best-known works, stage adaptations to existing dramatic texts. To a greater and greater extent, theater—*French* theater, but not only French theater—lost one of its key components: a text, a play. Directors tended to make up for this crucial loss by substituting other stage activity: dance, pantomime, movements of various sorts, organized or not, meaningful or not. And, unsurprisingly, this state of things led to generally devitalized writing for the stage.

If the place of the author hasn't returned to its former position of primacy, it has improved in recent years as French directors seek a perhaps more equitable distribution of attention to the various components of the work on stage, *including* the text. But even a modest return to the role of the playwright doesn't necessarily make for a revivified avant-garde. It all depends on what kind of writing, what kind of text you have, leading to what sort of theatricality. A Pirandello, a Genet, a Beckett expressed a radical theatricality that invited directors to provide innovative stagings *required* by the written work, inscribed in it. Today one looks in vain for such a need for experimentation.

During the final years of the last century and the early years of this new one, French dramatists and directors have been drawn to political and social content, ranging from French problems of immigration and integration to worldwide concerns with AIDS, terrorism, and American military domination. There is no reason why such matters cannot be expressed in theatrically experimental forms. In the 60s and 70s, the creative strength of the work of the Living Theater, of Richard Schechner, of Jean-Louis Barrault (notably in *Rabelais*), to name just a few, proved that political content and experimental form presented no contradiction and made for a particularly dynamic avant-garde. Now, the most theatrically stimulating works based on political and social reflections are undoubtedly those of Ariane Mnouchkine's Théâtre du Soleil, yet even these highly original stagings no longer qualify as "avant-garde." They are part of the best, the most inventive contemporary French theater, hailed around the world. Le Théâtre du Soleil (like others) has come a long way; it can now address massive audiences and be fully understood, despite its use of strikingly antirealist theatrical forms. But if an avant-garde is, as Ionesco rightly claimed, a frontal attack on what *is* with the intent of destroying it and replacing it with a new, radical vision, not even Le Théâtre du Soleil can be considered to be an avant-garde in the twenty-first century.

DG: Do you think that an avant-garde in the French theater today is even possible?

TB: The question came to a head in 2005 at the Avignon Theatre Festival. The festival's directors, Hortense Archambault and Vincent Baudriller, had selected the Flemish mixed-media artist Jan Fabre to lead the festival as that year's guest programming artist. The co-directors and their "artiste associé" succeeded in alienating audiences with a polemical, vulgar, ultra-violent program that sought to shock—hardly a novelty in 2005 and not even a successful attempt. After all we've seen, after nudity, incest, murder, rape, and cannibalism, what's left to try to shock an audience with? What horrors can you show them that they haven't seen daily on the evening news? Jan Fabre thought that urinating on stage, for instance, would be one way. The intellectual and aesthetic poverty of this strategy apparently escaped the festivals' directors who claimed to want to question the limits of theater, but it didn't escape the audiences. They were less shocked than irritated and bored. Theater was elsewhere.

One of the healthy signs pointing to a hoped-for recovery from the dismal current state of theater is this new refusal among audiences and critics to swallow anything and to endure everything. The emperor's clothes were new, and glamorous, and attractive—but perhaps their luster has faded. A few years ago, *The New York Times* theatre critic Jason Zinoman reviewed Peter Handke's splendid forty-or-so-year-old play (thus, no longer avant-garde, but possibly still splendid) *Offending the Audience*. Referring to the actors, Zinoman wrote: "As much as I tried to get into the far-out spirit, these cuties just couldn't offend me. It's really not their fault. Times have changed..."

DG: What do you think of the potential legacy of an avant-garde?

TB: The trouble is, in fact, that you can't bring an avant-garde to life again. The very idea is self-contradictory. Earlier in 2008, an interesting conference in Paris examined the major theatrical avant-gardes that succeeded the Theater of the Absurd, namely the brilliant New York avant-garde of the 60s and 70s, which was itself nourished by major non-American seminal figures such as Grotowski, Peter Brook, Tadeusz Kantor, Luca Ronconi, Andrei Serban, and others. The New York avant-garde earned world-wide acclaim and influenced theater and performance (as a new theatrical field came to be called) in many countries, and especially in France. Many of these theatrical avant-gardes emanating from New York relegated text to the background: The Living Theater, Richard Foreman's Ontological-Hysteric Theater, Richard Schechner's Performance Group and The Wooster Group which grew out of it, and Robert Wilson (to name only the most famous). Other equally inventive collectives, groups, or directors retained a greater—but still modest—link to text: Joseph Chaikin's Open Theater, the Mabou Mines, Spalding Gray, Peter Schuman's Bread and Puppet. One might mention, outside New York, California's inventive Teatro Campesino and the San Francisco Mime Troupe.

These various theatrical enterprises not only stunned the downtown scene in New York, they performed all over Europe and left indelible marks in France, Germany, Holland, Belgium, Austria, the Scandinavian countries, and Italy—and to a lesser degree in Britain, Spain, and Poland. The Living Theater, the most politically engaged of all, had its heyday in the 60s, culminating in their disruptive, agit-prop performances (or were they "happenings"?) in Avignon in 1968, that probably hurt their host, Jean Vilar, more than their intended target, the "establishment." Still, artistically speaking, this was the very spirit of the avant-garde. Efforts to revive The Living Theater's productions, twenty, thirty years later or more, were inevitably doomed to fail, precisely because you can't reanimate an avant-garde. Bob Wilson's stunning visual, wordless, ultra slow-motion early experimental productions such as

Deafman Glance introduced an entirely new "vocabulary" to what theater is. Thirty years later, his lavish productions, still visually virtuosic, are firmly part of the best of establishment theater. It's wonderful, it's admired, but it's *déjà vu* (literally); nothing new there.

DG: What conclusions do you draw from that?

TB: So what? So nothing. Simply a way to underline that the avant-garde doesn't stay in place. At the conference in Paris I mentioned, Richard Schechner, the head of the Performance Group and a guru of the avant-garde, recognized that the American avant-garde is no longer "avant"—that it has now become a tradition. In its heyday, he claimed, it was high in innovation and modest in excellence (a debatable point); now, in its assimilated days, it is, for him, high in excellence and low in innovation. Twenty to twenty-five years is the life span he feels avant-gardes have in general, and that would seem a reasonable estimate.

The fiasco of the 2005 Avignon festival may well have signaled the high-water mark of theater that scorns text. Yet even if one might therefore predict a gradual revalorization of the dramatic text, such a pendulum swing would not inevitably harbinger some incipient avant-garde, and in fact it isn't likely to do so. The years of revolutionary Theater of the Absurd followed by a period of directorial innovation shook up the establishment, as avant-gardes are intended to do. If an avant-garde is successful (and these were) it is absorbed, as I have suggested, by dominant forms, bringing on new established models of theater. Eventually, this new establishment (once it becomes, in Ionesco's words, a new tyranny) will be brought down by some new avant-garde. But the French theater isn't there yet. It's impossible to guess what such a new avant-garde might be; if it were imaginable it would already exist. But it does not.

What seems to be missing the most are playwrights— playwrights who have presented and staged significant texts that could, of course, include major innovations in staging. But the French playwrights seem to have abandoned the stage for television at the moment and to have been replaced by directors. Directors have become the new playwrights, and so many productions are not presented *by* an author but *d'apres*, *after*, an author, and what happens when the text is adapted or renewed is not the work of a playwright but that of the *director*, whose name often replaces that of the original playwright. This phenomenon, so common in France and Germany right now, isn't present in the United States or England. We'll have to wait and see which system generates the next important avant-garde movement.

DG: Is there a historical parallel to be drawn here?

TB: A similar situation existed in the nineteen thirties. Figures such as Aurélien Lugné-Poë, Jacques Copeau, Charles Dullin, the young Cocteau, the Surrealists, Gaston Baty, and Georges Pitoëff had led several decades of successful radical reaction against the realism institutionalized by Antoine, and a period of assimilation had settled in with Giraudoux, Montherlant, Anouilh, and Sartre. Who could have imagined while watching, say, Giraudoux's *Intermezzo* in 1933 that twenty years later, two tramps would wade through endless silences while waiting for Godot and that the Martins and the Smiths—interchangeable, two-dimensional pseudo English couples—would hurl phrases, words, and syllables at one another while no soprano, bald or otherwise, made a promised appearance. Beckett, Ionesco, Genet, and all the others had to write, to create, before their attack on the French theater establishment could as much as be envisaged. Only then could their avant-garde be detected, named, analyzed.

It's hardly imaginable that a new avant-garde won't eventually take form against the current theater establishment in France, in the U.S., or elsewhere. But what it will be and whether it will be successful, as the Theater of the Absurd was, or relatively unsuccessful with no strong long-term traces (as was the case, for instance, with the Expressionist theater of the 20s in France), is another matter. We'll need to be patient in order to find out. Theater companies are currently experimenting with technology, with visual effects, with a focus on the body, always in the absence of text. Some of the current work is really interesting, such as that of the Ivo van Hove and TG Stan group working in Flemish, and Romeo Castellucci, working in Italian—though in both cases the language is strictly incidental and mostly inaudible and incomprehensible.

But somehow one fails to detect the really new, the radically new, the blow to the solar plexus that forces you to take notice, grudgingly or not, and say WOW. But it will come again, sooner or later, and when it does, it is likely to stem from unexpected sources and take unusual directions. Where it will come from and what it might be, we certainly cannot know now. But it's a safe bet that it won't be a replay of the past… it won't resemble past avant-gardes.

DG: Can you relate this to other art forms?

TB: With respect to the novel, the Nouveau Roman was the last successful real avant-garde movement in France. Since then, individual authors have attempted and at times succeeded in developing experimental forms but in the absence of any movement. Meanwhile, the only important literary movement to stand out in France since the Nouveau Roman is Autofiction, which isn't an experimental movement—although it does feature numerous outstanding writers such as Serge Doubrovsky, Camille Laurens, Philippe Forest, Catherine Cusset and a number of others.

The odd man out is the art world. There the perspective has entirely changed and no longer resembles the erstwhile 'traditional' format of innovation followed by absorption. Now the market has taken over and the ever-present need to 'sell' an artist has created a permanent avant-garde linked principally to what collectors will spend, what auctions will yield. That has put the art world in a place of its own, a realm certainly beneficial to the artists riding the crest of the wave but not at all reassuring with respect to the innate quality and innovation of the 'new' artists and their new work. The link between theater and literature in general on the one hand and the art world on the other—so productive in past years—seems arbitrary and unproductive in the early years of the twenty-first century.

Journeys

DG: Your affinities with the avant-garde began very early: when you started teaching at NYU in 1956, you shared an office with John Ashbery. That's a fine start to your story with the avant-garde...

TB: When I defended my thesis at UC Berkeley, I was invited to teach at Harvard. But I didn't like the idea at all—the department was very complicated—so I went to NYU, where I had studied as an undergraduate. I met John Ashbery, but I wonder if John Ashbery couldn't just as easily have said: "I've just met Tom Bishop." John Ashbery wasn't famous at all. He was nothing. We were both nothing.

It was the university that had assigned us the shared office. They brought us both in and said: "Your desk is here. Your desk is there." And we chatted with each other for a year. He was my colleague, and I was his colleague. No one had planned it: not me, not him, not the university. We kept in touch: he came to speak here about Beckett, and of course he gave us the preface to *Ways of Re-Thinking Literature*.

DG: It seems you actively began to seek out the avant-gardes in the early 1960s. When did you first meet Beckett, whom you were very close to?

TB: I met Beckett in the early 60s. I was reading Beckett, and I was very drawn to his writing, which spoke to me on all levels. I hardly need to tell you why: the writing was overwhelming and I was overwhelmed; his writing told and refused to tell at the same time. I went to see him in Paris through my friend Alain Bosquet, who also introduced me to Ionesco, for that matter. I am very grateful to Alain for opening the door to Beckett, who wasn't easy to get to: Beckett wasn't a very sociable person; you had to look far and wide to find him. He had entered my field of action. He was already a big name, but a big name who was approachable. I approached him, and he allowed himself to be approached. We met up at the Closerie des Lilas, and then we went to La Coupole. He wasn't very talkative; I didn't really dare to speak either. It was the beginning of a relationship that took time—decades—to develop, but I wrote a lot on him. I directed the *Cahier de L'Herne* that was devoted to him. I organized conferences… I was very happy to do it, and—in so far as I could—I did it well.

This allowed me to meet Beckett, and it turned out we had tremendous things in common…

DG: What things?

TB: What things, ha! How can I put it… It's difficult.

Over the course of our meetings, our rapport became—slowly at first, and then more and more fully—a rapport of knowledge and friendship. We understood each other. That's also what allowed me to write on Beckett, on Beckett's work, which I never would have allowed myself to do if I hadn't known him. I allowed myself to do it because Beckett's work had become familiar to me, and I could speak or write about it with a fair amount of accuracy, thanks to my conversations with him.

DG: Would you send him the things you were working on so he could read them, so he could tell you his thoughts on them?

TB: Partly yes, and partly no, because I would also save them to show him when we saw each other. We saw each other relatively often, since I came to Paris often. I could always see him when I came to Paris. He was always available to see me. And so we established a kind of rapport, a friendly rapport that became a friendship.

DG: What was his relationship to New York?

TB: We spoke of New York of course: he didn't like New York, so coming to New York was unpleasant to him. And yet the reception of Beckett's work in New York was unique: Beckett became known very early in the United States, right in 1945. You didn't need to make the Americans 'discover' Beckett.

In sum, one might say that Beckett came to New York once, but he came without coming; he turned his back on New York. He came but he didn't like it. It was at the time of the première of *Play*. He didn't like the city at all.

Beckett was discreet, modest, but also very open: you could speak *to* him *about* him; he wasn't embarrassed by that. For my part, I was very eager to compare my impressions to the ideas he had of his own work. I've written a lot on him, as you know...

DG: Were you eager to collect what he said?

TB: I was eager to speak with him, but I didn't really make an effort to keep what he said, as you seem to be doing with me at the moment. I didn't collect what he said in order to go and make a book of it. We would speak. Beckett spoke readily of the staging of performances, or of pieces he was making and adapting for the radio or television. People don't often speak of this, but he took part very early in what were, at the time, new ways of making things.

DG: When you spoke, was it to shore up your impressions? To shore up your work, your analysis?

TB: In my work, I took into account the things we'd said between ourselves, and I do mean *between* ourselves: it wasn't just what Beckett said but what I said too. We'd speak with each other... And then there were the things said *around* us, during all the conferences that we organized and that were among the first contributions to Beckett scholarship. In 1981, for his seventy-fifth birthday, I organized a great celebration, with conferences, readings, performances, projections. He had given me his permission, and it all came together. Two months of events. I think he was fairly pleased with it.

DG: You even named your dog Beckett…

TB: Yes, and the one before that, Godot. In fact, Beckett—the dog—once bit Ionesco, the writer.

DG: Alain Bosquet had introduced you to Ionesco as well.

TB: Yes, I met Ionesco in the early 1960s. For me, he was an heir to Pirandello, on whom I had written my thesis. Ionesco was very pleasantly approachable, and I remember many a conversation with him. We met up in New York and Paris for years, and we'd speak of what was happening in theater. I often invited him to give talks and readings at NYU. *Rhinoceros* was a great hit on Broadway: the play had emerged from experimental playhouses—off-Broadway—and reached a large audience. He was very well known, and he received a lot of press, and at the same time he didn't make any compromises. His reflections on theatre and art contributed a lot to my own.

DG: Had you already started inviting thinkers and writers to NYU in the 1960s? Or did that come a little later?

TB: Yes... I'd invite people who embodied a form of modernity that interested me. There wasn't any kind of plan. I didn't invite them to represent a form of modernity, but that was what stuck.. The case that immediately comes to mind is that of Robbe-Grillet. He came to us for thirty years—and when I say us, I mean New York University. This was a period when he could show the students his own perspectives on his work—as you know, he had stopped writing, at least officially. I can't count the number of dinners we had together at the B Bar, beside the Bowery.

DG: The relationship continued: in 1982, you organized a conference: *The* Nouveau Roman, *Thirty Years Later.* You were one of the first people to inscribe the movement in a kind of literary history.

TB: Yes, I invited Robbe-Grillet—who was teaching at NYU—Sarraute, Pinget, and Claude Simon to have a dialogue with French and American professors. The authors were still very much active, but it was clear that the movement now belonged to literary history, and that the issues that the Nouveau Roman raised were in fact the same issues that all the literature of that era—or perhaps even of the twentieth century—had raised.

DG: It seems to me that, over the course of your journey, you've made some choices... Robbe-Grillet rather than Michel Butor, for example.

TB: Robbe-Grillet had a precision, a conciseness, a rigor that I didn't necessarily find in Butor. But I was very interested in Butor as well. I forget how many times he came to New York, but he came here. Robbe-Grillet was the Nouveau Roman's great author. But of course he wasn't the only one.

DG: There was Nathalie Sarraute as well.

TB: Nathalie Sarraute was huge for me. And I wasn't wrong about her. Jérôme Lindon was important, too, in this adventure of the Nouveau Roman.

What counted for me weren't only the people who were important 'in their own right,' so to speak, but also those who came, those who wanted to come to New York. For instance, Nathalie Sarraute didn't come very often. But I knew Nathalie even before she became one of the authors of the Nouveau Roman. I was already very interested in her work. I got to know, admire, and truly love Nathalie Sarraute's work before she really began to figure as a Nouveau Roman author—as she later did indeed… I was on very friendly terms with her. My wife and I would often visit her in the countryside at Chérence, and a true bond formed between us, but not in the sense that the things I wrote about her have the imprimatur of truth, not at all. It was simply that we had had the occasion to share the same experience. Nathalie Sarraute carried with her a very important life as a writer, and she like to speak of it: she liked to speak of what she was doing, why she was doing it, how she was doing it. She considered her work as a writer to be something open: I made the most of it, as they say.

But I wasn't the only one she would speak with: first of all, there were other Americans and other English people she could speak with—though not many other French people. She was very happy to speak with me and, let's say, fifteen or twenty other people about her work and what she was looking to do in her writing. She was very open about it, and this led to discussions and, I believe, to writings on her part. It was pretty wonderful.

DG: At the time, you were already a kind of specialist in *contemporary* literature.

TB: Yes, absolutely.

DG: That was fairly rare at the time: a professor working on contemporary literature.

TB: It was less unusual in America than in France. In France, it's true, one didn't write on contemporary literature—on what was in the making—or at least not at university: one had to wait until the people were dead. That was the difference between 'criticism' and 'research.' But that wasn't the case in America, where the distinction didn't carry the same weight.

DG: Do you think the literary worlds of New York—

where you lived—and Paris were completely distinct, or were there connections? Apart from yourself, of course.

TB: There were certainly connections. It was a brilliant period for French literature and culture: from Sartre and Beckett until the 1980s, the 1990s. From theatre to philosophy—at each moment there was a particular appreciation for what was happening in France. At one moment it might be Beckett, at another, Ionesco… And then there was a more philosophical aspect. Of course, some very interesting authors never had the career in America that one might have hoped for. Pinget, for example, never had a great career in America, or in France for that matter, but scholars have enormous appreciation for his work. He is an important writer. I invited him here, but it didn't necessarily take hold. That was also the case, for instance, with Philippe Sollers. Sollers was at the height of his glory in Paris, in the early 1980s, and we invited him here. It didn't work at all. I liked the early Sollers, the breadth, the originality of his vision. Even his formal experiments, like *Paradis*, interested me. But as for Tel Quel and all its wanderings, from Blanchot to Maoism by way of Structuralism—it just wasn't my thing.

On the other hand, Julia Kristeva met the expectations of American students; she addressed their concerns. She is a complex thinker, a generous person.

People often speak to me of Robbe-Grillet, but there too, it wasn't planned: it took me a while before I invited him; I had to come to believe it would really be useful for us to have him with us for an extended period. He came, and he greatly impressed the students. I invited him once, and then that multiplied and became a settled thing.

I'd seen and liked his work as a theoretician at Cérisy and other meetings of that sort. I'd heard him speak wonderfully. I was very impressed with his skill as a speaker. He was both a writer and a theoretician.

People don't realize it, but what I had was the ability to offer him a space where he could speak, and to pay for his trip and hotel. Hardly any more than that. But it worked well…

DG: Could you tell me about your invitations, about the way you went about inviting Alain Robbe-Grillet, and also the impact it had on the students?

TB: It worked with the students because speaking with them came naturally to him. His classes were always full, and he worked hard. I'd realized before inviting him what a hard worker he was. The words he spoke in class were very important to him, and he didn't make any distinction between the things he wrote and the things he said aloud. For the students, it was marvelous to be in the presence of someone so loquacious and so willing to speak with them. A wonderful professor.

DG: And that was at a time when he had stopped writing, officially.

TB: Yes, but he had also opened up a whole new path with his practice of autofiction: it was an opening that allowed the writer to speak, like a link between his writing and his thought. It was rare to see that, and he did it very well. OK, towards the end the autofiction got fairly bad, but in the beginning it was really serious work.

When I began to be interested in Robbe-Grillet—when I met him, read him, studied him—he had already written novels. He already had theoretical works but he also had creative works as well. The two worked very well together. It didn't keep working so well for very long. He became a better writer of theory than of literature. But what can you do—that's how it is.

That relationship between theory and fiction interested me a great deal. It wasn't a matter of choosing one or the other—both of them interested me equally: they complemented each other and created a sort of tension, a convergence and divergence. It wasn't *only* literature, if you will.

DG: Robbe-Grillet was an author who was also interested in cinema: throughout your experience, Tom, you weren't only interested in literature and philosophy. You were also interested in theater and the visual arts.

TB: I started early, in the 1950s, so when the 1960s came around I was already acclimated to a certain modernity, which allowed me to like certain things and not others. I certainly liked nearly everything that was French, and over the years I developed a great friendship with many

French directors: Jean-Louis Barrault, Ariane Mnouchkine, Peter Brook.

But I was also aware of what was happening in New York. Bob Wilson is someone I hold in very high regard, and I liked him a lot. I met him long before he was in Paris. Others went to Paris and made a name for themselves over there, but that wasn't the case with Bob Wilson. When he went to Paris, he had already built a tremendous reputation in New York.

I first met Wilson when I had a theatre group—I'd formed a theatre group for avant-garde theater. The invitees were composed of actors and theater people I'd collected in New York—mostly in New York but also occasionally from elsewhere—and I worked with Wilson at that time. For me, the Maison Française was a space for creativity, though it didn't remain that way. There was something dynamic there—and the Maison Française remained highly dynamic for quite a number of years. Bob had staged a theatre piece, or parts of a theater piece, at a theater in New York, and to make me happy he did a version of it at the Maison Française.

DG: What was it about him that you admired?

TB: Bob Wilson was tremendous—it was a completely different language, a language of spoken literature: the *word* counted, in the body. It was difficult to describe. But the word was there and you could hear… you could hear the actors *playing*, but playing in way that no one played anywhere else. It was very special and very highly appreciated, because it was a spoken language, but one that didn't really correspond to anything that we knew.

DG: And were you also interested in the whole underground performance scene in SoHo during the 1960s? That was something you went to see—the performances of Joan Jonas, of Charlemagne Palestine, of Simone Forti…

TB: No, not systematically. I saw a few, but my world was more the theatre world. Tadeusz Kantor I really liked. His pieces were true *mises-en-scène*, and it was very clever work, very precise work. The theater was very lively, and one had the impression that one was in the presence, here, of a *living* theatre, it was *alive*.

DG: What did you prefer, the New York theatre scene or the French theater scene with Jean-Louis Barrault? What was your relationship to each?

TB: It's difficult to say, because if you mention Barrault… I was a great, great admirer of Barrault, so of course I'll opt in favor of Jean-Louis Barrault. I went to see him at the Théâtre du Rond-Point, and before that at the Théâtre de l'Odéon, and at the Théâtre d'Orsay, in the building that would became the museum where you now work. Barrault was able to create for more than fifty years. It's admirable.

But it wasn't the only thing going, and, to be honest, I didn't have to choose. No one forced me to choose between Jean-Louis Barrault and Bob Wilson, or between Jerzy Grotowski and Antoine Vitez, or between the Wooster Group and Patrice Chéreau.

Really, I have a hard time answering you because these aren't questions that I asked myself—do I prefer what's being done in Paris or what's being done in New York… I had the advantage of being able to enjoy both.

I'm trying to think of a possible equivalent to New York theater… Fernando Arrabal's work, for instance, was much closer to theatre. It was truly theatre, rather than some new thing. I was very interested in him: his pieces were dynamic, alive—but they were theatre. But I also invited a number of theatre directors to come and speak and work in New York. I also acted in Virginia Woolf's *Freshwater* at the Théâtre Renaud-Barrault, with Nathalie Sarraute, Alain Robbe-Grillet, Joyce Mansour, Eugène Ionesco, Florence Delay… The actors were authors. It was the talk of the town, and it's one of my very beautiful memories.

DG: Rumor has it that you would fly to Paris once a week.

TB: No, no, I don't think I ever had a week like that, but I went often. It was possible for me to go to Paris often, and I took advantage of it. Perhaps five, six times a year, at least. For me, Paris was an absolutely necessary opening onto many things, and I took advantage of it to go and find myself at home again in Paris. I also tried to keep informed about what was happening in New York. The two went hand in hand. We also invited many American authors to speak at NYU Paris in relation to French literature. In 1982, we invited Toni Morrison and James Baldwin together for a conference in Paris. That was something, to be on stage with the two of them.

DG: I'd also like to ask you about your relationship to the visual arts: you have a great friendship with Christo; a great friendship, I believe, with Arman…

TB: Yes.

DG: What was your relationship to the artists, the contemporary artists, of those years?

TB: Very patchy, and rather belated, I'd say. The artists I liked were, I have to admit, already part of the era. Christo, for instance. When I liked Christo, Christo was there to be liked. There was already a great trend to like Christo, and so I liked Christo. I wasn't very original.

I've certainly been original about quite a few writers, but I'm not sure I was really original about artists. I don't think so. We cared about art—very early we also invited Harald Szeemann, Pontus Hultén—but it wasn't our specialty.

DG: And you did exhibitions with artists at the Maison Française.

TB: I did exhibitions—well, *did* is a bit much—I helped organize exhibitions with people I appreciated who were also my friends: they would exhibit at the Maison Française. Like Paul Jenkins, for example, and Arman. When I came to like Arman or when I set up exhibits for him— he did some great ones with me at NYU—he was already doing exhibits; it wasn't really any great original impulse. Or it was for me, yes, but not for the public. General art audiences were already very familiar with him.

DG: That brings me to another question. I've been trying to think of the type of profession you have created… You are a university professor, you direct a research center, a center for studies. But what you did, at root, was a little like what we now call curating—you were a curator of exhibits, of programs. It was also fundraising, because you were very skilled in that practice, and at the same time you are a university professor. What is your profession?

TB: Listen, for me, I was first of all a university professor. If someone asked me: "What do you do?" for me the answer was very simple: I'm a university professor; I teach; I give classes, university classes, classes in my fields. That is, I didn't give classes on Arman. I gave classes on Beckett, on the Nouveau Roman. The artists could find place in this because they had a place in it, of course, and they interested me. But first and foremost, I had a subject that I lectured on, and other subjects that were connected to it.

DG: But at the same time, Tom, a great part of your oeuvre consists in the conferences you organized, the exhibits you organized, all the things you developed in terms of organizing.

TB: Possibly, but those were extensions of my work. If you asked me, as you just did, how I defined myself: it was through Robbe-Grillet and not through Arman. It was through writing and not through painting. And it was through my own writing, my own research, more than it was through organizing. That doesn't mean I didn't develop friendships in the business world or in public life. Still, that wasn't the core of my profession.

DG: What's the connection between the work of a scholar and the work of an organizer? Between giving a class on Robbe-Grillet and inviting Robbe-Grillet?

TB: There were several ways of inviting Robbe-Grillet. I could invite Robbe-Grillet to come and speak of his oeuvre, or else I could give a class on Robbe-Grillet, and I myself could speak about Robbe-Grillet, and I could make the students work on Robbe-Grillet and we could work *on* his oeuvre. And for me, that's what my real work was.

DG: And the rest wasn't your real work? Everything you organized, everything you set up, everything that made you an impresario?

TB: No, that wasn't my real work. No.

DG: Really?

TB: It wasn't my real work.

DG: All the intellectual life you created between Paris and New York? All the things you were known for?

TB: I'm very happy about it and I think it was important, but it isn't what really mattered to me. Inviting Robbe-Grillet to speak couldn't be the really key thing for me, it couldn't be the core of what I was doing.

DG: OK.

TB: My goal in life wasn't to make Robbe-Grillet speak. And I mention Alain here, but that's true of all the other people I invited. I wanted to get people to think, and I wanted to contribute to the life of the literature and philosophy of my time. That had to come first of all through my own writing, my teaching, my research. I liked sharing this with the generations of students who came to us to discover something new, and who were ready to open themselves to new ways of thinking.

DG: And what about establishing bridges between New York and Paris?

TB: Yes, definitely, but that's somewhat vague, and it has to include research. I had the good luck to be living at a moment when New York and Paris were two global centers, and I took advantage of it. That allowed me to do positive things that I didn't do with Montreal or London. It never even crossed my mind. I think there was something special about these two cities, divided by an ocean but fascinated by each other. Hence the phrase I once used: *Le Passeur d'Océan* [The Ocean Traveler].

DG: Figures like Susan Sontag and Robert Silvers—your friends—were bridges as well, like you.

TB: It was a small world: we would meet up. Susan Sontag lectured with us. I was very good friends with her. She did work based on Barthes, who was teaching with us. One shouldn't imagine that everything was monumental and difficult. It was fluid.

Bob Silvers was probably one of the best bridges between American and European culture. These bridges existed; they were strong and significant. I wasn't alone... They allowed writers to take advantage of what they had made, and this encounter opened things up, it was open.

Thanks to my friend Robert Badinter, I used to organize NYU luncheons at the French Senate. People saw them as moments of political influence, but they were also an occasion for me to bring together this French-New York world. Each year, in New York and in Paris, we would honor a great trans-Atlantic figure: Frederick Wiseman,

Jean Nouvel, Isabelle Huppert, Louise Bourgeois... We would present them with a medal designed by Paul Jenkins. That created connections, naturally. At the Paris luncheons, a community would gather together, people from very different backgrounds: scholars, philosophers, politicians, publishers, diplomats. It was a lovely meeting each time.

DG: And how would you describe the New York intellectual world of the 1970s, 1980s?

TB: It was quite fragmented. I spoke of theatre; you spoke of performance—two different worlds. Perhaps that was the case in Paris too. After all, one couldn't speak of *the* intellectual world in France. It didn't exist. There were many different worlds, intellectual or otherwise—artistic, intellectual, with various sympathies. They were at once fluid and manifold. We once invited Richard Avedon to celebrate Roland Barthes.

DG: And what were your own worlds, Tom?

TB: My worlds were, first of all, the university world. I had created a very solid world around myself at the university—recruiting people for the department, teaching literature—and that involved constant work for me; you couldn't do it once and for all, you had to keep redoing it, updating everything all the time in Paris and New York. Richard Sieburth, Eugène Nicole, Denis Hollier, Philippe

Roger were all colleagues for years. One has to realize the number and the range of recruitments we constantly set in place: professors, guest professors, speakers for the Florence Gould Lectures… You were one of them, for that matter.

But I believe I can say that the New York intellectual world did not write the same before and after the Nouveau Roman. The Nouveau Roman changed things significantly: there had already been the impact of Ionesco and Genet, and of Sartre and Camus before them—great names, well known to some people here before you could really quantify them and say, "Here's a great network of intellectual thought." It was more open than that.

DG: Let me come back to curating: as you know, there's a great trend today toward curating exhibits, toward organizing programs, going out and raising money, and building relationships with the world that academics are rarely in a position to have, and that they weren't at all in a position to have in your time.

TB: Yes, that's something I did all the time, but it wasn't my profession. Fund-raising, for instance, came pretty late. I didn't start raising money for my work right away. I put some energy into it, and I had the good luck to find partners. Florence Gould initiated me in the art of patronage. She was very generous, and she did a lot for NYU. She also taught me many things: the annual luncheons at NYU came out of the ones she organized to support us.

We carried on with the tradition, in a way. Jean Riboud, the chairman of Schlumberger, was also a great support, and a friend. We were well supported. I didn't see that as a negative thing; it was a part of the whole, like making sure that everything is ready in the room when one organizes a lecture. Nevertheless, I didn't think of it as an end in itself—it was more of a condition.

DG: In the 1960s and 1970s, what would come to be called French Theory first appeared in America: Foucault, Baudrillard, Virilio, Deleuze, Derrida, Cixous… What was your relationship to that movement—if it was indeed a movement?

TB: It was a movement, and a very important one at that. French Theory was very present, and it dominated the literary and other discussions of those years. People would read writers for their theoretical content, without paying much attention to the theory itself. In other words, theory had won out, but it wasn't really studied for itself but rather as an interpretative framework. This might be a little rude, but even to this very day I'm not sure that people really know the specific work of each one of these authors. We organized numerous events on the Nouvelle Critique, on French Theory, on Deconstructionism: each step was celebrated at NYU from the 1970s up until the early 2000s.

DG: Who are the authors that particularly interested you in that group, or let's say in that current?

TB: I was very interested in Deleuze. I read Deleuze closely. I invited him; he came to New York of course. They all came to New York. I had particularly strong ties to Deleuze and to Derrida. Derrida was a true friend— I had a very, very strong intellection and personal connection with Derrida, who often came here. Less so with Deleuze, but Deleuze interested me greatly as well. We taught a lot of Deleuze's work, and he came here several times.

DG: And Foucault?

TB: Foucault too.

DG: Did you like Foucault? Or was he perhaps a little too 'radical' for your taste?

TB: I think Foucault is perhaps a little too something for me, but not too 'radical.' I can't imagine I'd judge an author by that standard. You know, I knew Genet, who would speak to me at length about the Black Panthers, a group he was strongly defending at the time, though he backed away later. As far as being radical is concerned, Genet was far beyond Foucault. Genet even came here and gave a lecture on revolution, surrounded by Black Panther militants. So, you see, as for radical things...

DG: So Foucault is too *what*, for you, Tom?

TB: He's very intense, isn't he... Every time you read Foucault, you can see him poring over his own oeuvre, and all you retain is simply the look in his eye—intellectual of course—as he pores over his work with those critical, intense eyes. I know he's left a rich legacy, but, for me, once you've found the 'catch,' it all becomes a little sterile. Foucault watches himself being Foucault. He thinks he's some kind of guru, speaking about things he shouldn't be speaking of, committing so many errors. I like his great books—*The History of Sexuality* or *The Order of Things*—and I fully appreciate his desire to be in dialogue with students, but his temperament isn't for me. He undercut his whole method.

That isn't the case with Derrida at all. Derrida approaches the text, the reading, the interpretation. He doesn't reject the fact of being personal, but at the same time he's much clearer. Hélène Cixous, too. I read her with great interest. She still enthralls me. I think she found a good way for text to open out onto text, onto her text. Hélène's texts are worth the effort it takes to approach them, to understand them, to read them—with great interest, and with an open mind on the reader's part.

DG: There's another question I wanted to ask you Tom, about your connection to French politics. How did that first begin?

TB: At the Maison Française, very early I began to invite the political figures of that period. Antoine Pinay was one of the first. But I think things really got going with Pierre Mendès France. I invited him to give a lecture at the Maison Française. His integrity was admirable—like Robert Badinter's, and actually the three of us met up once together. Pierre Mendès France's lecture on modern democracy made a huge impression. The room was packed; it was a very great success. Afterward, I organized a dinner in his honor at NYU. I was very moved…

DG: You also invited Raymond Barre, at the time when he was prime minister, to give the inaugural lecture at the Institute of French Studies, and today you are still close to Marie-France Garaud, among others… But during the Mitterrand era it was said that you were one of the closest people in the world to François Mitterrand, in New York at least. Jack Lang was a great friend of yours… And of course Robert Badinter, whom you remained very close to. What was your relationship to power at that time?

TB: Power, in those years, had finally come to the Socialist Party. It was a great political moment. I think France was the first country to become truly socialist. I can't see any others that were openly socialist at the time. I was on close terms with the French government in a way that I now consider to have been less positive than I thought. The relationship wasn't as close as I thought it was. What bound us together wasn't *political*, strictly speaking.

I spoke with Edgar Faure, whom I knew fairly well, and François Mitterrand came to open the celebrations for the bicentennial of the French Revolution. For me, it was a great moment—to have invited Mitterrand and to host him. Louis Malle gave a lecture, Francois Mitterrand delivered a great speech and he received an honorary doctorate. He said beautiful things about us… But I recognize now that the whole thing was less brilliant than I thought at the time.

We had many, many political interactions, some of which were interesting—namely, the political things I did with Mitterrand and Jack Lang, for instance. I invited each of them to speak. I gave them a platform, and that gave *us* a platform too. When I gave Lang a platform, for instance, it was a platform *at NYU*, it wasn't any random place, and during the 1980s and 1990s we were the place where French politicians wanted to have their voices heard in New York. And New York, at the time, was America. So it wasn't nothing… I have to say that we also cultivated relationships on the American side with politicians who loved France. We honored several senators on both sides of the ocean.

DG: Some, like Robert Badinter, became close friends.

TB: Robert and Élisabeth are longtime friends. Élisabeth's thought has had a very great impact on the world, which isn't an easy thing for such a complex oeuvre. Robert is a great friend: I deeply admire his strength of character and his sense of the public good. What he did for the abolition of the death penalty is historic. But he's also a very powerful intellectual.

DG: You had a rival at Columbia in Michael Riffaterre, your counterpart.

TB: Relations were relatively bad. And in so far as they weren't utterly bad, we accepted each other. Riffaterre was a very intelligent man, but, *but*, he walked a hard line that led straight to himself. There wasn't a Columbia line. Today there is one—Columbia is much improved. It was a bit like now with Trump, where everything has to go through Trump. Well, everything had to go through Riffaterre. His official line was himself. It wasn't a political line; it was mostly an intellectual line that led to his writings, to the books of the people he was publishing at Columbia and with Gallimard. He had collected some interesting people, a Columbia fan club. That was never my method.

DG: And what about Semiotext(e), the magazine and the publishing house that Sylvère Lotringer directed while he was at Columbia—what did you think of it?

TB: Semiotext(e) has always interested me, because I think Lotringer had something. In fact, we invited him to NYU in the 1970s. He had just arrived at Columbia. He was very intelligent, and his intelligence wasn't dogmatic or merely academic. He saw—he sought out—openings, connections between things. If things were happening at Columbia, it was thanks to Lotringer. I've always admired that. Even if I didn't always like what he was doing—that didn't matter. Looking back on it, it was a truly interesting initiative. In fact, Baudrillard was an author who was close to Lotringer and who often came to NYU, particularly to speak about September 11th with Laure Adler.

DG: Another figure who was dear to you was Roland Barthes...

TB: I was lucky to have known Barthes well. What I loved about Barthes was the extent to which he *gave himself.* He was open; he was free; he wanted to speak; he wanted to please. But I don't mean *to please* in the sense of doing nice things, but rather in the sense of living up to expectations. And he always lived up to expectations, I think. I invited him several times. He came to give a lecture, and then several lectures. There was an understanding between him and his audience that was difficult to explain, but very beautiful. He was happy to be speaking. One had the impression of a self-gift, that Barthes was giving himself to the audience, and that's quite rare. It's quite rare to see someone who has the desire to pass something on through their words, a desire to pass on their thought. And he did it with such joy; it was really quite remarkable. I've rarely seen that in a person, and I've rarely seen it in a professor or philosopher. In fact, I wonder: did we have the impression of being in the presence of a philosopher? Not really. It wasn't really Barthes the philosopher who was speaking, it wasn't a discourse where you could speak of *him* and *us*. It was simpler. He came as a guest professor, and a whole new generation of scholars came with him: Philippe Roger, who attended Barthes' seminar, also came to New York all through the 1980s.

DG: You met many people, Tom: what was the impulse behind these encounters?

TB: I certainly didn't meet everyone. But I met the ones I wanted to meet. I made choices. And Barthes, for example, was one of them. I wanted to meet Barthes—I was looking to meet him. And I wanted to know Beckett, of course, and others too. Each time, there was a desire on my part. And this desire was intense and real. Which means I wasn't looking to meet people to be able to say: "I met so-and-so," and I wasn't looking to meet people just to talk. I saw Barthes in Paris quite a few times before he came to New York. I saw him in Paris when he was teaching there, and he came to speak to us after he had come to speak to me. But speak *to me* isn't the right way of putting it. He didn't come to speak *to me*—we spoke *together*. I think that's the right word. He liked young people, and he liked speaking. He felt at ease.

DG: You would choose the people you wanted to meet, and then you would go and meet them.

TB: I wasn't looking to meet everyone; I was really looking to meet the people who might interest me. That's what I mean when I say I made choices, nonetheless.

DG: And how did you make these choices—what were your criteria?

TB: Listen, it might sound ridiculous, but what interested me were interesting people. In other words, people whose writings—and perhaps spoken words too if I had heard them—interested me, and of course this was quite a varied group of people, potentially. That's why we were able to invite figures who each had radically different approaches or came from radically different fields.

DG: But still, your choices reflected a kind of concern for the avant-garde, for a certain modernity.

TB: No, not a *concern*. It wasn't theoretical or programmatic: I was in Paris often; I'd go to the Festival d'Avignon; I'd follow what was happening at the Festival d'Automne—all the gatherings that make French artistic life what it is. And what we were doing was articulated around conferences: that's how we started with Serge Doubrovsky in the 1970s, with a major conference on Proust and the Nouvelle Critique. We had Serge, Leo Bersani, Gérard Genette, who often came to visit us.

DG: You didn't invite too many conservative historians of literature to NYU.

TB: No, I can't say that I did. But still, I invited—we invited—some people who were certainly more conservative than the people I liked, though that was usually for a particular reason, because they were there, because we could get them, we could have them make NYU a part of their trip.

Incidentally, I didn't only invite people who might interest me, but also people who might interest our department. That's important. Things weren't completely personalized.

DG: How do you explain that New York-Paris relations were so personalized in the eyes of the intellectual world, especially in France—that everything seemed to be centered on you? Someone once told me that Philippe Sollers considered it to be your fault that things didn't work out for him in New York. For a time, people thought that New York was Tom Bishop.

TB: Well, I did take up quite a bit of room, after all. Philippe Sollers' reaction was false, of course, but typical. Philippe was turning in circles around his group, wasn't he, so he could speak about it, he could introduce his students to it. But he introduced it poorly. It didn't work. I had no part in the fact that it didn't work; it didn't work because *he* didn't work, because what he was doing wasn't working.

Philippe Sollers was at the height of his glory; it was at the time when he was the most famous. And so things worked for him because he was Philippe Sollers. People came to listen to him speak. But it didn't work because he was out to give them an idea of himself. He was at pains to introduce himself to them, to give them an idea of who Philippe Sollers is. He was too self-centered, and the students, the audience, didn't want a vision of Philippe Sollers—they wanted a vision of the world.

Philippe always, always, always looked out for himself, and it didn't do him any good. Which is a shame, because Philippe is someone who had a lot of merit but he never let go of himself; he retreated into himself, and it didn't do him any good. And then, starting with *Femmes*, he let himself get caught up in a *Parisianisme* that eventually did him in. His skill was still there, but not much else. As a matter of fact, the university presses that had taken his earlier books didn't clamor for that one, or for any of his books since.

DG: You are very good friends with Bernard-Henri Lévy, whom you were the first to invite to the United States, in 1980, when no one in New York really knew of him.

TB: He was already a phenomenon in France. He was the talk of the town in Paris: Barthes had paid tribute to him. He may even have already been an editor…

I invited him to give a lecture. And it turned out fairly painfully because the lecture had to be translated—he had a student next to him translating what he said—and then he started translating himself, but he translated himself badly, and so the information didn't really get through to the students, and on top of it all they took issue with many of the things he said. But he has such charisma that he drew people to him: it worked; the audience went with it. The audience understood that they were in the presence of someone larger than life. And therefore they had to follow him. So they tried to follow, with great difficulty: he managed to carry them along with him, even if they didn't really understand what they were being carried by.

There were a certain number of events with Bernard in the years that followed, and he gradually made himself understood. So it was only a beginning, but the beginning worked well. It was the very beginning of his American adventure. He was here again only a few years ago.

DG: You were also well acquainted with the media…

TB: It's true I'm conscious that if no one knows what you are doing, it doesn't exist. I was fortunate that the French newspapers covered what I was doing in New York and Paris: *Le Monde* often ran stories on our events. And over here I collaborated with *The New York Times Book Review* and wrote a certain number of reviews, especially on contemporary avant-garde literature. In France, I closely followed *L'Observateur*, and Jean Daniel was a friend of mine. As with Mendès and Robert Badinter, I have a lot of respect for the ideas Jean Daniel championed, for the positions he took. But to get back to your question, one can approach the problem of the press from different angles: let's just say that people belong to a milieu, and when you set up operations and have the good luck to see the press take an interest in them, then that allows you to have even more impact.

DG: What is less well-known to people, Tom, is that you were among the first to welcome the post-colonial in French-language studies. You invited Assia Djebar right from the 1990s, first as a guest lecturer, and then as a professor.

TB: Absolutely. Assia had already taught a little bit, and it was clear she taught postcolonial literature. She was an important author in her own right, and she championed this approach with great energy, talent, and volubility. Her words were always intelligent and flowing. She spoke easily: she was at ease.

DG: How did the invitation come about?

TB: It took me a little while. Assia Djebar came to give lectures at first, and then I invited her to come and join the department. When I say, "I invited her," it's true that I was the one who invited her, but no one is ever alone in inviting someone, and the department was in full agreement to invite Assia Djebar. And so the department sent out a formal and very open invitation, with truly unanimous support. Denis Hollier in particular was very favorable to the idea.

DG: But why was it important?

TB: It was important because we had the impression of being in the presence of someone who could travel widely—which she did: she traveled very widely, and she gave a lot of herself; she spoke right and left, at NYU and elsewhere. And she made postcolonial literature known— I mean a *certain* postcolonial literature, not postcolonial literature as such, which is a problematic essentialization.

DG: And why was it important to include Maghrebian literature in French-language studies. Why was it important to you?

TB: Well, it was important because we had come to a point where it was clear that this literature needed to be represented, needed to be heard. It was clear that things had changed, that postcolonial literature is an important literature, and we wanted to keep listening to it and furthering it. And that's what we did, until other universities began to follow in our footsteps, much later in some cases. Toward the end of the 1990s, we also celebrated Edouard Glissant and *Métissage* in a great conference that Maryse Condé participated in, along with many other figures. At the same time, we invited Gayatri Spivak to speak of French Theory.

DG: Speaking of the department: you had the reputation, Tom, of being very authoritarian.

TB: Really?

DG: Do you think that was the case, or not?

TB: I spoke with authority, but was I authoritarian... Probably. I don't believe I was, but after all, if people say so, I have to believe I'm wrong. What can I say? The truth is that I always wanted the department professors and the guest professors to feel supported in what they were doing. They always had a place during the conferences I organized several times a year, and during the big annual conference. I can't recall a single conference that didn't have at least one NYU professor. It was also a question of giving life to the department, as much as I could.

DG: That leads us to the big question about the relationship between the Center for French Civilization and Culture and New York University.

TB: Listen, I directed the Center and I am a professor at the university. It was normal, therefore, to have points of alignment, and, on the contrary, it would even have been inacceptable *not* to have had them. For the conversation series that I set up with Olivier Barrot and that I was very proud of, "French Literature in the Making," each month we would invite a French writer who would come and present their work to a New York audience. Naturally, the Maison Française at NYU had a following, but it was also an occasion for our students and our colleagues to be in contact not just with history, but also with what is being done today. The goal wasn't to have certain events for students and certain other events for other audiences. Everything had to intermingle.

DG: We've spoken of your relationship with Deleuze, with Derrida, with Robbe-Grillet, etc. but that period came to an end around the 1990s, the early 2000s. You could have stopped there and said, "Whatever happens afterward isn't my problem: it doesn't interest me anymore." But you continued to grapple with contemporary literature. Why?

TB: Listen, it's difficult to answer your question except by saying: Why not? That's what I had been doing my whole life; it was my professional life, and my professional life hadn't changed. And it was going strong. So I don't see why I wouldn't have kept on with it during the 2000s: the guest professors, the conversations between French and American writers, the nearly daily lectures and performances, the discussions about art—which you yourself participated in with Philippe de Montebello, Joachim Pissarro, and Philippe Vergne. There was no reason to stop.

DG: Do you think the 2000s and the 2010s are as rich as the 1960s, 1970s, and 1980s?

TB: I don't think so. I don't think they are as rich, but that doesn't mean they can't become rich again. At the moment, they aren't rich.

DG: Why not?

TB: For a long while, I could go to Paris and meet up with friends, friends of friends, and get a feel for what was being made. Today, that's impossible: we were one of the first departments to bring in Caribbean literature, but that isn't enough. Thought today is happening in Africa, in India, in Latin America. It often comes from discussions that wouldn't have been possible in the 1960s, but the richness I'm speaking of isn't the richness of a single place anymore. I don't know if it ever was, but at least it felt like it.

DG: Do you think that the status of French literature has changed?

TB: Yes, it's true, and it's a major sign of relative weakness. The French language is weaker today than it used to be. I won't deny it—it's clear. I don't like it. You can see it in all the departments. To re-energize the French language, you have to open it up.

DG: I'd also like to ask you about NYU. What was NYU's place, and how has it changed over the years, up until today? Especially in regard to France.

TB: Well, NYU's place in regard to France is enormous. It was enormous because I worked very hard to make it enormous, and to make it remain enormous. It was something I did consciously: I worked at it. A lot of universities are creating centers all over the place, but fifty years ago

NYU Paris was a new thing, and we did a lot. We did a lot to make NYU Paris a quality program, and to make NYU Paris a place that would attract students. We created partnerships between our programs and the Festival d'Automne, France Culture, French newspapers… Denis Huisman was a great friend: he had a foot in both worlds, and we set up some summer courses together at NYU Paris with the schools he had founded.

But if you compare, for instance, the 1970s or 1980s with today, you can see a pretty clear drop in the number of students, and it doesn't show any sign of reversing… Interest in France has dropped everywhere; there's nothing you can do about it. And we've seen that literature isn't doing well in the university today, in the *universities*: all the Romance languages—French, Italian, Spanish literature—they are all doing poorly.

The students aren't listening anymore. They don't study literature anymore. It doesn't interest them anymore, and of course that's a source of enormous regret to me. I spent quite a lot of time fighting this decline, which I now believe to be an established thing, a loss. Literature as a whole is going through a difficult period, here and elsewhere, and that's true at the Collège de France; it's true everywhere. It's not just an issue limited to American universities.

DG: Do you think the relationship between the intellectual and academic worlds has changed?

TB: It has definitely changed. The intellectual world has definitely changed: it has shrunk, and what I'm saying now—that literature departments are losing ground at universities throughout France, the U.S., Italy, everywhere—is true of literature in general. Literature as a whole is declining everywhere. It seems as if the fluidity that I tried to establish between research, creation, the university, and various media is a thing of the past.

DG: Do you feel you belonged to a heroic bygone era?

TB: Bygone, yes—I think it's bygone. I wouldn't say heroic. It wasn't heroic; it was fantastic. To participate in the great age of literature was wonderful; it was very fine. You have to keep in mind that we were addressing audiences of students who were passionate…

Was it heroic? We didn't have to be heroic to participate in it. We were lucky to get to participate in it.

DG: I think it was also a question of character. There's a quite interesting parallel to be drawn between you and Robert Silvers, the legendary co-founder and director of *The New York Review of Books*. Bob passed away in 2017; he was eighty-nine. You, you're still in great form; you're ninety years old. You're going strong, and he was going strong. There's a very special energy that not everyone has today. And Bob had the same energy—and the same curiosity, in fact.

TB: Yes, I can definitely see some similarities between Bob and me, and they both point in the same direction: the continuation of something that has been very strong up until now and that we want to carry forward—both in our own relationship to life, and in our vision of the things we are fighting for. I think that's the goal we both have; that was the goal we both had.

DG: Absolutely. In a way your work at NYU was also that of an artistic director, inviting people, commissioning texts... The Florence Gould Lectures, the volumes you edited, the conferences you held at the university—all of these testify to your work as an artistic director, as it were.

TB: Yes, that's true. That's completely true. In fact, I served as an artistic director from time to time at festivals.

I agree with you that we did a true large-scale creative work, not just on French literature, but on many kinds of literature—of *literatures*. It wasn't limited to France, and it worked best when it brought people together. For us at NYU, this was a relatively long and powerful era—a very long and powerful era. We understood that *métissé* literatures had things to say that would reach a general New York audience. It wasn't only about the university, even if many things came through the university and left very dynamic traces of themselves in their wake. And that's something positive that has remained, within the university and beyond.

One wonders what remains of it all—when I'm feeling pessimistic, I'm not sure that anything much remains of it at all, anywhere. One wonders about one's legacy—or I wonder, in any case.

DG: Do you have any regrets, any authors you think you overlooked or should have invited more often, any people about whom you say: "I missed out on that author."

TB: No doubt, I must have missed out on a few. But you know, the way you put the question seems to imply that I used to choose this or that person instead of another. That wasn't the case at all: some people would come often; it worked well; other people came less often; some people didn't come at all. It wasn't simply a question of an arbitrary choice on my part. It depended on the students and, of course, on the guests themselves. And who was I to say what was right or not?

DG: Don't you ever say to yourself: "If I had invited such-and-such a person, it might have worked."

TB: Perhaps. Perhaps. But if I ever said that sort of a thing to myself, I got over it pretty quickly. So I can't answer your question.

DG: As I've told you, the things you've done seem to belong to a kind of heroic age of thought and action. When Robert Silvers passed away, people said: "There can never be another Bob Silvers after Bob Silvers." In the same vein, do you think there could be another Tom Bishop after Tom Bishop, or is it impossible?

TB: That's a difficult question you've put to me. First of all, an ensemble that was positively inclined toward poetic and intellectual creation would have to be possible, which isn't the case today. Literature isn't strong enough today; it's weak; it needs to fight for its survival. I'm not speaking merely of French literature, but of all literatures and of the way they are taught at university. Literature departments are weak in relation to other departments.

And a new intellectual situation would have to arise in universities or in whatever will take the place of universities. The things I was able to do depended on the possibility of having speakers from the literary world, or from public life, come to the university without a problem. I'm well aware this might seem self-centered, as if I were saying: "things would have to be how they were before."

Perhaps things shouldn't be how they were before; perhaps things should be completely different. That's a fundamental question. The conditions that allowed this creative work aren't necessarily the conditions that would allow a future creative work. It's easy to say: "Well, first, you would have to have strong literature departments; then you would have to have strong universities defending literature." But that's all based on the current state of things, or even on the past. I'd be telling you that things have to be how they were, and that's obviously wrong.

But who knows what turn things will take? Perhaps literature will become something very alive in a much larger sense, easier, more approachable, less segmented than it is now: perhaps the relevance of academia will become more and more limited, until it loses all importance. And in that case, and in that sense, so what? It won't be bad. But it won't be how it was.

DG: At NYU, for a very long time you also had nearly total autonomy. The Center for French Civilization was a kingdom within a kingdom.

TB: Yes, that's true. But it's true because I wanted it to be that way, and I created it that way. And it was the case within a university that not only tolerated but also favored such policies. But that was in the past: my first impulse, in answering your question, was to imagine that things should continue as they were, but it's impossible. Perhaps they have to continue in a way that's completely different, but I can't predict it.

DG: Are there things that you are particularly proud of, things that make you say: "Now that was a great success"?

TB: Yes, I'm particularly proud of the ensemble that we created at the university, the group of professors we recruited.

I keep coming back to your question. At first I said, "it would have to continue the same way," and perhaps it will continue some other way. But if you look at the contrast between how things are and how they were, I'm proud of what we did, I'm very proud. And I delighted in it. I had the good luck to live and experience it with interest and with a lot of pleasure too.

DG: Today, Tom, I know you've been thinking a lot about your childhood in Vienna. Do you feel Viennese, Viennese Jewish? Do you feel French, Parisian? Do feel like a New Yorker? Or all of these at once?

TB: That's a big question. First of all, I feel like a New Yorker: I am a New Yorker. New York, for me, is a thought-capital that I live in with joy, and with sadness now that I see it all declining—I almost said *collapsing*, but that's false, it isn't collapsing. But it's going down and down; it keeps going down. For someone like me, who saw New York when it was active, alive, when everything was the subject of the most open conversations... It's sad.

As for Vienna, I don't give a damn about Vienna. I'm not drawn to Vienna in the least.

DG: And what about your Viennese Jewish identity? Not the Vienna that became a Nazi city, but your Viennese Jewish identity? The world of Freud, of Musil, of Karl Kraus, of your family?

TB: Yes, I'm fond of all that. But it's so far away now... I'm a Viennese Jew but I am a completely non-Jewish, non-Viennese Viennese Jew. So for me the whole thing contains an internal contradiction.

What replaced Vienna? I have no idea. Vienna is still there; Vienna replaced Vienna. One person's Vienna was replaced by another person's Vienna, but it's still Vienna.

DG: You are a New Yorker; you are a non-Jewish, non-Viennese Viennese Jew... Are you a Parisian?

TB: Ah! Parisian, yes, definitely. I'm definitely Parisian, and I am passionately Parisian. I love Paris. I love being in Paris. I love Paris because it's my city. It's my city where I feel marvelously at home. From New York University Paris to the Flore, to those streets I've walked through for decades, where I've seen so much of life, where I have so many friends.

DG: More than in New York?

TB: No, not more than in New York.

DG: Same as in New York?

TB: Different from New York.

DG: Are you American?

TB: American, definitely. But being American is very difficult sometimes. Simply look at Mr. Trump and dear Mr.

Trump's activities. And then you'll understand just how difficult it is to be an American. But I am an American, and I will remain an American.

DG: To come back to an identity we were speaking of earlier—Jewishness—do you consider yourself Jewish?

TB: Listen... I consider myself Jewish because that's how life works. They make you Jewish. They name you Jewish. They tell you, "Bishop," you are Jewish. Baumgarten, you are Jewish. They exclude you, and they name you.

DG: Bischofswerder, you are Jewish.

TB: Bischofswerder, you are Jewish... Which is quite funny, because Bischofswerder—my German name—is as Christian a name as Bishop. "The servant of the bishop": it doesn't get any better than that.

But still, I am a complete atheist—I have no religious thoughts whatsoever—so of course having to answer questions about religious affiliation seems quite artificial in the end: what does it mean? It doesn't mean anything to me.

DG: Beyond all of these—rejected or reclaimed—identities we've named, what are you? What are you above all, more than anything?

TB: I'm a New Yorker, much more than I'm an American.

DG: More Parisian than French?

TB: Yes, definitely. Though I don't say that against France, but rather for Paris. I've lived in France, spent time in France, but Paris is always the place I return to. This might seem old-fashioned, but there's an intellectual life in Paris beyond anything I've known anywhere else.

DG: You're not anti-French; you're pro-Parisian.

TB: I'm definitely not anti-French.

DG: How would you define yourself, beyond the categories...

TB: I think I've covered all the options; I don't think I've overlooked anything that I am. I'm American; I'm a professor; I'm French, Parisian. I'm both: French *and* Parisian. But I'm not Catholic, and I'm not Protestant. And I'm not looking to be.

DG: As we come to the end of this interview, is there anything you would like to add to all we've said? Anything we've forgotten?

TB: No doubt I'll have to call you in a couple days and say: "Ah, of course there's also... *et cetera.*" But I think we've already spoken of the important things like French, American, Parisian, *et cetera*—spoken of them quite enough even—and I don't think I've forgotten anything important... important to me that is. Important to the world is another matter entirely.

LIFE

DG: How much do you think literature has changed over the many years you have been engaging with it?

TB: The nature of literature is never fixed: it is very, very changeable. That's all right because people should change and they do change. Literature cannot be considered to be separate from the world, separate from people. I do not want to say it simply mirrors it; that would not be accurate. I think literature is a voyage of discovery. I have discovered a number of people through my work here. I'm sure you have too.

DG: When you invited me to organize a conference with you at New York University's Center for French Civilization and Culture, I immediately thought of "re-thinking literature," an issue which, I think, you have tackled all along the way.

TB: Well, I don't know. What do you do to rethink literature? One of the things that our life has taught us here is that we bring people together. We bring together people who work on literature, on exciting literature, on different literature, on new literatures that aren't the same things we've been working on all these years. We are into new things.

I happen to have spent a lot of time thinking in terms of the workings of the books and writings of the avantgarde. The avant-garde as a way of approaching literature, of approaching thinking has appealed to me over the years a great deal.

That's what makes literature what it is. That's what brings people together, whether they were Rimbaud at one time or, for that matter, Rabelais, to stick with the odds. That's what I'm interested in. That's the phenomenon of the literary element, the literary presence that fascinates me.

DG: You've been very pluralistic about it. As you say, a lot of the people that you have supported or been close to hated each other or hate each other. How can you be that pluralistic? Go from Derrida to Houellebecq.

TB: Now you've put me on the spot. Go from Derrida to Houellebecq. Wouldn't you rather go from Derrida to somebody else? I'm very fond of Derrida and I'm not very fond of Houellebecq, even though it was a normal thing for me to invite him, quite early on, at NYU. I'm not interested in defending Derrida at the expense of Houellebecq. It's too obvious.

DG: Let me make the terms of the equation even more complicated, and bring in two of your close friends: from Samuel Beckett to Pierre Bergé, the business and life partner of Yves Saint Laurent. You were able to bridge those gaps…

TB: OK. That's a tricky one. I'll keep Samuel Beckett for later and reply on Pierre Bergé.

Pierre Bergé, whom I knew well and loved and respected, and who was an extraordinary human being, was, of course, not a great writer, but he was an extraordinary impresario, an extraordinary illuminator of literature.

He helped endorse literature, and he endorsed damn good literature. That doesn't mean everything he endorsed was always great. But that's not important. You don't have to be 100% in your stamp of approval. What's important is the direction you're moving in and what you're looking for.

What you're looking for is new invention, new thought, and good new thought. I will leave the comparison which I was trying to get away from before… I'll leave it gotten away from because I'm not interested in knocking a writer.

Bergé supported, and I mean supported in a very strong and serious way, many writers of different kinds, but many writers who were outstanding writers.

When you think in terms of what happened in the field of… I was going to say French literature but it's not just French literature: it's art and culture. Pierre Bergé didn't limit himself to French literature. The literatures that Bergé supported over the course of his lifetime were multifaceted, manifold. They contributed immensely to the advancement of culture in the world. Not simply in France, not in any one country, but in the world.

DG: I have a final question for you: You are an incredibly energetic and vibrant almost ninety-year-old legend. Today, what do you see yourself as, mainly? Do you see yourself as a scholar? As a writer? As a cultural impresario? As a blend of the three? Or anything else?

TB: I have trouble answering you because I'm not in the habit of having some kind of a description of myself for myself. I really don't know, and it doesn't interest me.

DG: What interests you?

TB: What interests me is life. To be simplistic about it… I would say life. I let myself in for this, you called me a ninety-year-old, etc., which is true. In another two months I'm going to be ninety. I wish that in another two months I was going to be twenty-two. I would prefer that but that's not the way it is.

I don't spend my time worrying about it or thinking about it. That's not what concerns me. I'm not concerned about my age and I'm not concerned about age.

I am concerned about living life to the fullest possible. I would like to have a chance to stay fully alive and conscious until the very end of my life. If I could have that, that would be a great gift. I don't know why anybody should give me a gift, but if I had that, that would be good. I would like that.

Each of these conversations came from a specific moment: the first was held in French at the Palais de Tokyo at the invitation of Jean de Loisy and Claire Moulène on July 9, 2018; the second—in English—was in preparation for Tom Bishop's foreword to the volume we co-edited, *Ways of Re-Thinking Literature* (Routledge 2018); the third—in French—took place at Tom's apartment on Mercer Street on November 16 and 17, 2019; the fourth, in English, at the Albertine Bookstore on Thursday November 8, 2018.

The French conversations were translated by Peter Behrman de Sinéty.

1st edition

© DIAPHANES,

Zurich-Paris-Berlin 2021

All rights reserved

ISBN 978-3-0358-0366-2

Layout: 2edit, Zurich

Printed in Germany